Dear ALPHA FEMALE

IT'S NOT HIM. *It's You!*

AN INTERACTIVE DEVOTIONAL DESIGNED
TO HELP YOU ATTRACT THE LOVE YOU DESERVE

By

CHRISTAL D. JORDAN

DISCLAIMER

ISBN E-book: 979-8-9876171-0-6
ISBN Paperback: 979-8-9876171-1-3
ISBN Hardback: 979-8-9876171-2-0

DEDICATION

This book is dedicated to all resilient women who refuse to give up on love. Even through your previous heartbreaks and pain, you are still determined to win at love. I am in awe of your strength.

To all the alpha females who have unmet deadlines of love and are wondering if you are worthy or if it will happen for you: you are already enough and worthy of happiness. I pray that you let God exceed your expectations and persevere to give love another try.

Everything I will ever do is for my heartbeats—Chanelle Edryce & Stone Erickson—my husband, Adrian, who taught me to love again; my mother Jacqueline Jordan; and Aaron Jordan.

For I know the plans I have for you, declares the Lord, "plans to prosper you and not to harm you, plans to give you hope and a future." - **Jeremiah 29:11**

If you adhere to the ideologies associated with Alpha, Beta, etc. traits in both male and female personalities, chances are you've been led to believe that an alpha female shows certain domineering and aggressive behaviors.

Alpha women have been described as being bossy, manipulative, sexually voracious, condescending, and emasculating, but those are usually traits exhibited by people who desperately want to be in control, but aren't.

A real Alpha female may have a strong personality, but what makes her a leader, what inspires her diligence and tenacity, is a strong sense of self, and of purpose. - A Conscious Rethink

(Winter)

This book is about love between a man and a woman that leads to marriage. While I recognize relationship goals can vary, I am a married alpha female, and I am speaking to the alpha females who desire marriage.

Table of Contents

FOREWORD

Being loved is a basic human need. As women, we must learn who we are and what we need before we look for partners. So many people are unhappy because they didn't take the time to love, heal, and get to know themselves before starting new relationships. Christal and I have had countless conversations on love and relationships, and I'm glad she wrote this book and included God's word in the relationship conversation. Success and material items mean nothing if you operate outside God's will for your life. I know Christal truly believes in love, and we both want other women to experience the kind of love God intended for all of us. **- Rozonda "Chilli" Thomas (TLC)**

INTRODUCTION

Have you ever asked a woman what she wanted in a man, and the length of her list made you wonder if said man existed? If you haven't, chances are you are that woman.

DEAR ALPHA FEMALE

Although we've drawn a mental picture of this streetwise yet cultured, college-educated, seven-figure man with the body of a former pro athlete who is willing to be 100% faithful and a fantastic provider—it's almost certain this unicorn doesn't exist.

Assigning our potential mate this list of controlled variables almost assures us that we are safe from the riff raff and ultimately in control of the outcome. Ironically, most alpha women with these unrealistic lists end up dating and falling for men who fall extremely short of what they claimed was non-negotiable.

IT'S NOT HIM. IT'S YOU

During my single years, I would talk to alpha females about what they wanted or thought they needed in a man. Their eyes would light up as they listed a litany of characteristics they almost proudly held as "dealbreakers" for a potential mate. Usually, those lists were so long that I'd narrow my eyes and think, "Wow, it's going to be hard to find him in this dating pool." I know this because I was this alpha woman, and I know many others.

Why is that? Women build unrealistic fences in pursuit of the perfect life due to unresolved pain manifesting. When you haven't healed, you create an atmosphere that is guaranteed to bring you exactly what you fear. Focusing on the flaws of others will only expose your weaknesses. Focusing on a veiled attempt to control your partner will undoubtedly result in a partner who uses your pain against you or a healthy man saving himself and deciding against wasting his time with you.

My colleague, a relationship blogger from *Little Black Book 91*, co-hosts an OWN digital relationship recap with me. While reviewing a particular reality episode, he pointed out this behavior: "Women who build extremely high fences set themselves up for failure because only dogs want to jump high fences. A good man of character sees the issues a mile away and excuses himself from the pursuit."

Happiness begins from within. When we face our past pain and allow ourselves to heal, we can honestly decide what we want in a mate and attract what we deserve. Once we uncover the part of us that is holding the right ones back, we will have more confidence, clarity, and peace.

Dear Alpha Female, It's Not Him. It's YOU: An Interactive Devotional to Attract the Love You Deserve is a love letter to the strong, accomplished, and proud female of the twenty-first century (a.k.a. "alpha female") who, despite her successful business track record, academic accolades, lavish lifestyle, and strong sister circle consistently, finds herself failing at romantic relationships.

Love cannot exist without accountability, and this book is, from one alpha female to another, an introspective opportunity for self-reflection in its rawest state.

ATTRACT THE LOVE YOU DESERVE

I wrote this book for the alpha females who are high-performing women chasing careers and accomplishments to replace what they lack. This interactive devotional is a tool for self-discovery and will correctly position you to remove the mask of happiness and, indeed, be happy.

I caution you not to wait to read this book; be open to creating a more suitable list for a mate and prevent your unrealistic expectations from causing you to end up with a man who is barely making ends meet or who is highly uneducated. Don't find yourself stuck with a jobless freeloader or a drug dealer with multiple felonies or end up settling for someone who doesn't match up to a third of your list, let alone the entire list.

It was the revelations in these chapters that brought me the transformation I needed and gave me love that feels better than I ever could have imagined.

I have a fantastic husband, family, and career. More importantly, I have self-love, and I know I also deserve love from others.

I invite you not only to read this interactive devotional but also to take action in your life quickly by answering and applying the self-reflections at the end of each chapter. True love does exist. This book will help you to be open and create a list based on what you truly want and not based on fear; then, you will be able to attract true love. I know this book will be a blessing to you.

from Christal, XO

Section I

It's Not Him. It's YOU

The Beginning of Love

When you close your eyes and imagine love, do you see roses on a bright and sunny day? Or are you consumed with the darkness of the clouds and rain? What's your love fantasy?

As young girls, we start with high expectations of love. An optimistic lens piques our interest. Once outside factors, time, and trouble arise, our expectations of love and ourselves are lessened, and our ideal love image fades. As a result, some girls become weak and easily manipulated. On the contrary, some girls become super strong, focusing on achievements to win love. I was the latter.

I was born in Ohio. At home, it was me, my mom, and my younger brother. Although my grandparents lived close and I enjoyed spending time with them early on, I was primarily raised by my single mother. After reflecting on things as an adult, I believe that mothers love their sons and teach their daughters. At the same time, fathers love their daughters and teach their sons. When the household is unbalanced and the burden is placed on the mother, as daughters, we feel a void missing out on a father's love, and naturally, we crave it.

My father was not around much, evident based on our finances, but the pain it put on my heart was immeasurable. I craved my father's love, and I became a daddy's girl without a daddy. I knew my father not being around wasn't my fault, but how could I make him love me? How could I make him come around more?

WORKING FOR LOVE

I did well in school, hoping it would get me more love and attention not only from my father but also from my mother. I was action-oriented, seeking love and acceptance, which followed me to adulthood.

I became more ambitious and driven. I didn't have limiting beliefs in my ability to perform well at school or work. I did my best to outperform and overdeliver in hopes of more love. When I got older,

I did the right things in life, but my love life didn't go the way I wanted. What's wrong with me? I wondered.

MY UNRESOLVED PAIN

My family dynamics shaped my real-life view of love. Due to the lack of love and finances, I dreamed about things getting better and having a husband and children in the future. I wanted to be a great catch, so I worked hard to achieve great things to position myself for love. However, after appearing on *Iyanla, Fix My Life*, I realized I couldn't work hard to guarantee love. Love starts with us accepting God's unconditional love and then loving and accepting ourselves. After my big aha moment and doing inner healing work, I met a wonderful man whose love I didn't need to work for. After dating for one year, he proposed to me, and we later married.

When I realized my problem stemmed from my unresolved issues from childhood and I accepted God's love, I attracted my knight in shining armor without working hard for it.

SELF-REFLECTION

Did your family dynamics shape your desire for love? What did love initially look like to you? What circumstances changed your original view of love? When did you start basing your worth on your accomplishments?

NOTES

NOTES

Love Lessons

Though I live high above in the holy place, I am here to help those who are humble and depend only on me. - **Isaiah 57:15 CEV**

"God helps those who help themselves" was one of my grandmother's favorite sayings. My mother worked, so she would drop me off at my grandparents' house, and I spent a lot of time at their house. It never replaced the love I craved from my father, but my grandmother showed me unconditional love. When she saw me, the smile on her face spoke volumes. She was excited just at the sight of my face. My grandfather, her husband, was equally loving to me. I felt safest with them, and I did not have to do anything to earn their love.

When I was four years old, my mother moved my brother and me from Ohio to Oklahoma, away from my grandparents. I talked to my granny on the phone, but it wasn't the same. I missed feeling loved. I knew my mom loved me, but her love appeared more visible for my brother. I felt lonely when we moved away, because I wasn't near my grandparents and I still wasn't seeing my dad.

After we left Ohio, I didn't see my grandparents until I was thirteen. I was so excited to see them. When I arrived at their house, I looked for my grandfather who wasn't there. To protect her finances, my granny left him, because she made the most money out of the two of them and refused to share it with an outside child. Her attitude was "he's gone; good riddance." And her outlook was "focus on earning your keep by working hard."

My granny was different than the more traditional women in the community. The traditional women in the community enforced love and respect, while my granny, an alpha female, focused on her strength in working hard. My granny promoted hard work. I watched my mother emulate her hard work, and I later followed suit.

ALPHA FEMALES & HARD WORK

I love my granny, and I am thankful for her strong work ethic. However, as women, we do not have to rely on ourselves. When we think we do, we keep working harder and harder. This teaches us independence as working women, married or single, resulting in a lot of pressure and stress leading to overachievements. We do not have to be overachievers to be loved. God wants us to lean on Him and not ourselves. When we know that our strength and joy come from the Lord, we trust Him more with our finances and our heart.

To dispel the old myth of God helping those who help themselves, try seeking God and relying on Him. This will help you to relinquish some of the control in relationships and be more vulnerable. It is okay to be more vulnerable. Our strength is not based on how much we can achieve on our own.

In the previous chapter, I asked what shaped your earlier view of love. Now consider strength. Where did you first recognize a woman's power? How did this shape your perspective on womanhood? For me, both love and strength were shown to me first by my maternal grandmother.

Notes

NOTES

IDENTIFYING SELF-LOVE

No one on our planet is the same. We all have unique fingerprints, blood, and other things in our bodies that set us apart from anyone else. I learned to work hard from my mother and grandmother. However, does hard work determine our worth?

Invisible Pain

Circumstances at home didn't cause me to have limiting beliefs about my ability to achieve greatness, but I doubted who I was and if I was good enough.

Where there is a lack of love within a home, due to pressure placed on one parent, developing self-love as a daughter isn't enforced. We don't learn to love ourselves, and we settle for awards and achievements because they help us prove our worth. For me, this is what my identity as a woman was based on and what led to me seeking love for the wrong reasons.

I always thought that if my dad was around, my life would be easier and my mom wouldn't be burdened. I also thought I had to be what I considered beautiful to be loved by my dad. On the one hand, I wanted to be in love and married because I never wanted to be poor; but on the other hand, I wanted to be loved for attention and to be celebrated. Thus, neither reason removed the lack of self-love that I had, and it led to me seeking validation.

MANIFESTATION OF UNRESOLVED PAIN

I had the opportunity to see my father when I was twelve years old, but I didn't want to, because my face had pimples all over it. I thought he wouldn't love me because of my acne. However, it was I who couldn't love myself because of my imperfections.

With my mom, it wasn't much different. I thought her love was conditional based on how I did in school. Love to me has always been contingent upon me achieving something or striving for perfection. Consequently, I set out to achieve greatness in my love life, hoping to find love.

Although I wasn't able to receive the love I wanted from my dad, I thought if I worked hard, then a man would love me. I wanted to get married, start a family, and enjoy life. After doing things the right way, my first marriage still ended. This was devastating, because I had finally felt safe with my husband, and I had trusted him to love me. My guard had been completely down, and I was completely let down.

When my first marriage ended, I was reminded of the rejection I felt from my father's absence. I was so hurt, broken, and lost. I could not control my husband's betrayal no more than I could prevent my father's abandonment. I focused on what I could manage, which was my career and achievements, which confirmed my self-worth.

After dating, in search of my new image of love, I had an intervention. Afterward, I was able to see myself beyond my achievements, and a fantastic man was able to love me unconditionally. I hope this book will be a tool for you to define your worth and eliminate the need to work for it.

SELF-REFLECTION

What do you love about yourself? Write a letter to your younger self and say everything you wished your parents had said to you as a child. Put your pain on paper and release any negative emotions about love.

Are my goals really what I want?

Can I rely on myself?

NOTES

NOTES

The Image of Love

Attention doesn't mean affection; attention doesn't mean love.

We live in the social media world with tons of filters and editing apps to make us appear how we want. In real life, we have wigs, makeup, etc. to help us uphold the "us" we want "them" to see. To show up as our authentic self, it takes self-love. It's not until we learn to love the picture we see in the mirror that we can feel real love from a man. Now that we've identified the importance of self-love, we must strive to love the unfiltered version of us we see every day.

It's All About the Image

I began my career as an entertainment publicist. It's my job to portray and protect the image of my clients' brands and ensure everything goes perfectly. My clients get paid based on their image, and people love them. Although their fans don't know them, they love what they see. This led me to further believe that I had to be viewed by men as perfect in order to receive their love. My self-value was based on my success and image. If I was at my ideal weight, then I felt good. I quickly showed up with confidence, because I liked how I looked. When my looks didn't meet my expectations, I felt less about myself, fearing how others would receive me—even my parents.

Over time and after learning to live with my new normal after getting divorced, I still had the desire for love and companionship. I continued to work hard in my career and hoped to meet a great man. I thought I was a great catch because of my career success. I thought I was the prize based on my accolades, but to my surprise, the men I met weren't impressed with that. The men wanted a different kind of woman. I was confused because I thought I was preparing to meet a great man, but I discovered men didn't love me for my accomplishments, and some were intimidated.

Now what? My dad couldn't love me, and my first husband proved the same. I've done everything possible and achieved as much success as possible, but why can't I find love?

It Wasn't Them; It Was Me

I later learned that it wasn't the fault of the men I dated; it was my fault. When I started to love *myself* unconditionally, instead of what I accomplished, I was open to *receiving* love unconditionally. Focusing on the essence of who I was turned out to be so refreshing. I never actually felt safe trying to uphold a particular image, because I always had to be a step ahead to stay on point. I now felt freer and like I didn't have to wear a mask. It wasn't until I let go of my "wife-type image" that I was able to accept myself for the woman that I am. I began embracing myself and showing up regardless of my weight.

When I met my second husband, I was amazed because I didn't have to pretend to be anyone but myself. He loved me for Christal, with or without my wig. After I accepted myself, someone else appreciated me. I love myself, so I can love my husband and receive his love.

Self-Reflection

What image are you portraying? If you view yourself as beautiful and worthy of love, that is what you will receive. What are the negative things about yourself that you have been battling? Write them down and get rid of them. You are made perfect, and love isn't earned or based on others' opinions. Self-love results from how you see yourself on the inside. What's your image of yourself?

Notes

NOTES

Career and Love

What's on your list? Is it a seven-figure salary so you can enjoy the Benz, designer bag, and baecation? Or is it a beard and abs to satisfy other desires? What traits does your ideal husband have?

As alpha women, we often approach marriage the way we do our careers. We set the goal, get the degrees, be assertive, and achieve our goal. Then we go after love the same way. We plan to get married by a certain age, get the degrees, be assertive, but then get disappointed when we don't meet the goal. This often makes career women in their thirties and beyond very depressed.

Career goals and relationship goals are different but can be applied the same for your benefit. The difference in achieving career and relationship goals is based on teamwork and other individual contributions. It's easier to get a job, because it's based on our own abilities. It takes our individual skills and experiences to receive promotions and new opportunities. Preparing for marriage, on the other hand, requires collaboration and agreement with little emphasis on our skills. We can't check all boxes to receive success in relationships like we do in the corporate world. Our goal of marriage can take months or years to achieve. Are you prepared to achieve your goal of marriage for the right reasons?

LOVE

It's not wise to approach love the same way you do your career. However, your unwillingness to settle in your career should be applied to your marriage journey. If you are unhappy with a job, then you go and get another one, because you have the skills to confirm you are qualified. If a relationship is not working, then you can confidently exit as well, because you have self-love and you know what you want; that qualifies you to be considered for the position of a wife. The key is to be confident in who you are. If you are, then your marriage goals will not be based on a biological clock, and you will be willing to wait for the best opportunity.

SELF-REFLECTION

Is your decision to get married based on societal pressures? Is it based on another achievement you want to get under your belt? Are you willing to try at love even though there is no marriage guarantee? You must be honest with yourself and know your walk away point.

NOTES

Notes

Redefining Womanhood

Because I am a woman, I must make unusual efforts to succeed. If I fail, no one will say, "She doesn't have what it takes." - **Clare Boothe Luce**

Why did women stop loving womanhood? Traditionally, women were more gentle and nurturing than they are today. The natural makeup of a woman is to be classy, from how she dresses to how she speaks. Women used to embrace their femininity and the things that make them unique. The older women would teach the younger women how to love and treat their bodies and just how special they were. Women were soft and open, and it was celebrated. What changed?

Birth of the Alpha Female

Growing up, my mom was a nurse, and she taught me cleanliness and proper hygiene. Nursing is a career where women can be more of their natural selves and focus on nurturing and caring for people. I started my career as an entrepreneur, where being feminine felt like a handicap because I worked in a male-dominated industry. I adapted to the industry that I worked in, as many other career women do. I became more aggressive to avoid appearing weak. I tried being more forceful to display strength. There weren't women in my line of work to counsel me as I saw the older women do while growing up. Femininity was considered a weakness, so I responded accordingly to be successful. As time went on, I became a leader along with my other women peers. The days of the traditional woman became a thing of the past, and the alpha female was born.

The alpha female is incorrect in thinking that setting records in her career makes her great. The alpha female isn't teaching younger women how to embrace sensitivity. Alpha females lead by example to prove they deserve a seat at the table and are chasing success. With the absence of the traditional woman, in conjunction with abuse and mistreatment, women face turmoil inside because we can no longer embrace who we indeed are. Women are not teaching from a feminine perspective as much, leading to young women being lost and unaware of the dysfunction within themselves. Femininity has been separated from our identity, which is why so many women cannot have loving relationships with men.

It's the man's job to love his wife, but if you are defensive and aggressive, are you showing men that you are lovable? God said for women to respect their husbands, but if you are guarded and overly confident in your ability, do you think men can see you as a potential wife? Will you help and respect him on his journey?

I've never been as domestic as my mom, so I overcompensated in other areas such as school and, later on, work. After getting divorced, I was more of an alpha female, and the example of a traditional woman was no longer in sight. However, the tenacity that helped me achieve my career goals was not the characteristic that allowed me to become a wife to my now husband. It was about balance. I had to adapt to my environment as an entrepreneur but not let my achievements define me as a woman.

EMBRACE BEING OPEN

Womanhood is the essence of being present and not in conflict with yourself. I stopped telling myself I had to be like men to avoid being hurt again. It still takes work to practice this, and I often must let my guard down and be more open. To remain strong and comfortable with who I am while celebrating womanhood, I learned how to balance my actions and emotions while being more open and vulnerable.

What's your feminine/masculine makeup? Are you more dominating and need to shift to bring out your natural instincts? When you can bring out your feminine side, it's easier to be who you are and to love yourself. After you define who you are and love yourself, you are ready to be loved by someone else. Being loveable is suitable for men. Alpha Female, if you put the trials and triumphs you faced aside, how can you redefine womanhood?

NOTES

Notes

SECTION II

DEAR ALPHA FEMALE

Femininity is part of the God-given divinity within each of you. It is your incomparable power and influence to do good. Be proud of your womanhood. Enhance it. Use it to serve others. **- James E. Faust**

Alpha Female

"Why are you such a bitch?" Have you ever heard that? Is your meekness your weakness? How do you balance your inner femininity with your outward strength?

Alpha Female

I came to terms with who I am. I am an alpha female. Alpha females aren't angry, jealous, or conflict-driven women. We are ambitious and professional women: doctors, lawyers, entrepreneurs, and other types of employed individuals. Everyone is happy when we go along with things, but we are judged more harshly when we speak up. The difference between an alpha woman and a problematic woman is that the problematic woman is always challenging. As alpha women, we aren't difficult for no reason; however, we do not trust easily, which can be a turn-off for men.

STUBBORN AS A MULE

My first horse was an Arabian Dutch Harness mix mare named Paris Hariq. I had to assert my dominance over her, and then she would become an obedient horse and submit to me. "She's a dominant/alpha mare," one of my equestrian friends explained. At the word, "alpha", I remember feeling a sense of dread, because when I was a single Black woman with a PR agency, it was a title I heard many times. It was usually stated as a negative trait, which described a woman being successful but alone.

After working with my horse Paris consistently for almost a year, she went from being resistant to barreling towards the gate with excitement at the sound of my truck. I put a lot of time and effort into making Paris comfortable. Once Paris started to trust me, she made all my efforts to win her over worth it, but it was hard work.

What I've learned from my experience with Paris is that once trust is developed, relationships with alpha females are much more manageable. Like Paris, when meeting new people, I could be read as resistant and stubborn, but the truth was that resistance was a sign of being uncomfortable and afraid. With my husband, I had to learn to trust him to make sure things were good. Trusting him made it easier for him to love me without feeling the effects of my stubbornness. Even now, it takes practice for me to trust him after being independent for so long.

As alpha women, we take time to adjust to people, places, and changes. Men prefer the more accessible version of us with less resistance. Just as I judged my horse as difficult before getting to know her, men judge us—and "alpha female" can sometimes be synonymous with "problematic woman." Consequently, at some point we have to let our guards down to put our femininity on display.

To have the relationship of our dreams, we must balance when to trust and when to be cautious, but still be open to change. Could you be coming off as too stubborn for men? Could you be warmer and more inviting while maintaining your level of comfort? How can you balance being open without feeling threatened?

Relationships are no guarantee. There's always a chance that we will get hurt. We must follow peace, control the energy around us, and take chances. Prayer is a great way to decide whether you are with a man who will nurture you or one who will tear you down. When you choose to be more open and allow your feminine side to lead, you will know how to balance your outward strength with your inner femininity.

SELF-REFLECTION

Think of a time when you were too hard on a man. How would you do it differently now? What do you want your future husband to see when he sees you? Focus on that and follow your heart.

NOTES

NOTES

PREPARING FOR LOVE

How can two walk together unless they are agreed? - **Amos 3:3**

Men are the hunters, not women. A woman can desire marriage, but traditionally the man proposes. It is important not to treat marriage as just another goal and be mindful of what you truly desire.

One of my initial desires for marriage was based on financial lack. Because my family struggled financially when I was growing up, I thought it was my dad's fault for not being around. I never wanted to be poor ever again, so my original view of my ideal marriage was one of financial security. However, after getting divorced, it wasn't his financial status that I missed. I longed for someone I could run to and feel safe with without judgement; no money could soothe my pain.

Before I began to work on myself, the lack of security in my life as a child caused me to yearn for a man to feel financially and emotionally secure. However, I later found that what a man could do for me wasn't enough. I wanted to be with a good person who was trustworthy. The healing work that I did made me realize this.

HIS AND HER LIST

Is your desire for marriage based on your dissatisfaction with yourself? When you are self-reflecting, you may find that your ideal man's image was based on your lack of something. Maybe it was a lack of finances, a lack of love, or a lack of protection. Once you uncover what's truly on your list, you have to make sure that you are also what's on his list. A couple's views on marriage have to be aligned.

When you are ready for marriage, you also must have a man who is ready for a wife. This should be discussed at the beginning of a new relationship. You can't expect to be the perfect companion and hope he will propose to you. You have to be sure it is you who he wants and for the right reasons.

SELF-REFLECTION

Create a new list of desirables for your mate based on who you are today. What are the non-negotiables? What will be your red flags? How will you know that the real you is who someone truly wants? You have to want similar futures. How will you make sure you want the same things? Does he want children? Are you open to this? Decide these things before going the distance with someone.

NOTES

NOTES

Faith in Love

Now faith is the substance of things hoped for, the evidence of things not seen.
- Hebrews 11:1 NKJV

A game show that I've always loved watching is *Family Feud*. The thing I like about the game is that the host will ask a contestant a question. Sometimes the contestant's answer seems so far-fetched that the host will turn to them with a look of doubt. However, I always admire it when the contestant, no matter how ridiculous the answer sounds to the host, points up to the board and says, "It's up there."

The reason the contestant yells out, "It's up there," is because they are speaking what they want to manifest. Their goal is to win $20,000.

To do that, they not only have to beat the opposite team but also make it to the bonus round. And sometimes the game will be tied, and they have to play an extra round for one last try.

Because the goal is $20,000 and it is a journey to get there, the contestants come prepared to put the work in. They speak positive words, huddle up in agreement, and collaborate so that their family can win. They do not stop if they lose one round, and they know that they may have to play an extra round. They keep the faith, celebrate the wins and the losses, and keep going to the goal.

Are you prepared to win at love? When I was single for ten years, I had doubts and feared I would never find love again and remarry. Like so many other career women, I would utter words of contentment and confirm that I would be fine with or without a man. However, my heart said otherwise.

When God sent someone to pour into me and I had a mindset shift, I didn't let fear win. I wanted to get married, so I started speaking it into existence. Within one year, my true love manifested, and now I am enjoying the fruits of my words.

What are you saying about your love life? Like you can believe in the controllable goals, such as buying a house and car, you can put your faith out there and believe in love, although it requires collaboration and partnership.

The process may not happen as quickly as you would like it to. If you give dating a try, then there is a possibility that it will not work out. However, you are striving for the ultimate goal, which is companionship, family, and happiness resulting from friendship, love, and marriage. Therefore, you may not win every round, and you may have to continue for a bonus round. However, be prepared to keep going until you achieve your goals and let your words follow.

FAITH

No matter how grim it may seem, God is up there, and He can do exceedingly abundantly above all that you ask or think. The next time you are in conversation about getting married or you are asked if you plan on getting married, your response should be, "Yes, I will get married," and look up and point to the sky, because it's up there.

NOTES

NOTES

ACCOUNTABILITY

Accountability is necessary for growth. When we examine our motives and actions when things don't go as planned, we allow improvement in the future. My marriage ended because something happened that I couldn't control. However, the lesson I took from my actions was to be mindful and more present.

Our upbringings determine our views. Both my mother and grandmother were single and ultimately gave up on marriage. I didn't want this to be my reality, so I watched shows like *The Cosby Show* and let them shape my view of what I wanted my life to look like.

In college, I got married to a great person. We had two and a half children, including our dog, a lovely house, a nice car, and seemingly the perfect life I wanted. Like the mother on *The Cosby Show*, I could have it all, including a dynamic career. I loved being a wife and mother, but often my career commanded my attention.

REALITY CHECK

During my first marriage, my goal was to ensure my family was financially straight. I wanted my children to have every opportunity I had missed as a child. I even wanted my husband to have the success I envisioned for him. I worked toward these goals and was focused on them for my family's sake. My determination for financial success was so strong, I believe it contributed to me missing things going on at home. I thought my marriage was solid, but I ignored signs of my husband's unhappiness. I was very alert and present once I learned of his affair.

Cheating is wrong, and there is no excuse to dishonor your spouse. Marriage is sacred. However, I couldn't change my husband's infidelity, and focusing on the details of the betrayal felt worse. I was stricken with grief and cried for weeks. Instead of blaming my ex-husband for the demise of our marriage, I focused on what I could do to improve myself in the future.

Lost Love

The lesson of lost love hit me hard and fast. This taught me that I not only needed to be in the room but also mindful of what was going on in front of me. I still use that experience to be more present for myself and my current husband.

In our careers, we are accustomed to juggling many things, but multitasking is not always the answer to success. I learned that success is maximized when you focus on what's in front of you. Consequently, you reap the benefits and are not blindsided by an overactive mind.

Measure Your Success

Are you present for yourself? Do you enjoy getting a pedicure, or do you answer emails simultaneously? When you spend time with your loved ones, are you present and in the moment, or are you planning your next career move? What are three things that you can commit to being more present for?

When I started to be more present for myself and in my relationships, it reduced the stress from focusing on so many things. It also increased my enjoyment of what was right in front of me. Will you be more present?

Notes

NOTES

FORGIVENESS

Be kind and compassionate to one another, forgiving each other, just as in Christ God forgave you. **- Ephesians 4:32**

If someone does something wrong to you, do you have to forgive them? Or do you act like they never existed altogether? Does it depend on who the person is?

As alpha females, we are not only accountable but also responsible. When we learn the rules, we follow them and are compliant. We know our role in life and what we are supposed to do. The problem is that this can cause pride and make us more masculine and unlovable when others make mistakes if we are not mindful.

Forgiving is not an option but a necessary skill for success in our careers. As alpha women, we know that forgiving will help us achieve greater heights within the workplace and personally succeed in what matters most: family life.

We learn to look the other way when we face racism or sexism. We stand up to defend ourselves when needed then move on. We do not dwell on negativity, because we know it will hinder our progress. As a result, we put up with a lot, routinely practice forgiveness, and keep striving toward our goals. We do whatever is necessary, whether exercising or going to therapy, to show up to work as the best versions of ourselves despite being wronged.

It's easier to forgive at work because we learn not to take things personally. Do we have to be forgiving in our personal life? The answer is yes, although it is not as easy.

My dad hurt me by not giving me the love and support he should have, and though it still hurt, I forgave him. I forgave him not only because I loved him but also because he struggled with addiction. Addiction is not an excuse to abandon responsibilities, but I chose to show him grace. I forgave him for the sake of my peace and ability to move past the pain.

Forgiveness in my personal life also went to my first husband. I forgave him for the betrayal, because forgiveness was necessary for my healing.

As accomplished women, pride can try and creep in, leading us to harbor unforgiveness. However, it is with humility that we are rewarded. When we forgive, we are sowing seeds of love and will reap love as a result.

No one is perfect, and all we can do is strive to improve daily. Although we cannot see others' intentions, it is crucial to give them the benefit of the doubt. I chose to forgive my father and later my husband. Forgiving them helped me to be more gracious with myself. Forgiveness is for the other person, but it is also for us.

Are you holding back forgiveness from someone? Are you ready to release resentment and replace it with love? You have the power to forgive. Exercise your power.

NOTES

NOTES

RISK VS. REWARD

You will either relish in his love or regret you ever met him. Is that how you view starting a new relationship? Does the uncertainty of the outcome scare you?

When you enter a romantic relationship, it is always an investment. You will receive a return on your investment, but it may not be what you are hoping for. If the reward of love outweighs the risk and you pursue it, then determine how much of your time, love, and energy you are willing to invest in the short and long term.

I was excited to buy my first house myself. Although the real estate market can be risky, I knew that buying a home aligned with my future and even my short-term goals. I would benefit annually, because the interest and taxes I paid for the house would reduce my taxable income. I also knew that as I continued to spend on the house, I would benefit in the long run with equity. Consequently, the reward of a paid-for asset at retirement would be far greater than the short-term risk of market fluctuation.

RISK VS. REWARD

In real estate, as long as you maintain your property and pay your expenses, you are almost guaranteed a positive reward in the future. Wouldn't it be great if relationships worked like that?

If we want a happily-ever-after marriage, we must decide when the risk of dating or pursuing a relationship is worth it. Get all the facts checked out and do your homework on him; give it your all if you think you will receive your desired outcome. Although it's a risk, you still have to go into it with confidence and no doubts.

If you are afraid to enter a new relationship with someone due to fear of getting hurt, then either that person isn't right for you or you are not ready to invest. Men want women who are all in. Don't enter a relationship if you are lukewarm.

At some point, you must risk your heart getting broken and the undesirable feeling of another failed relationship if the potential mate has qualities that will give you the long-term commitment and short-term companionship you want. As alpha women, we don't ever hesitate to invest in our careers or our businesses, because we understand the 10,000 hours formula. We have faith in the law of sowing and reaping when it applies to business, but we doubt when it applies to love. We even chalk up losses at work to "the process." As an entrepreneur, I made many mistakes, lost money, and invested in my company without proof of a return, yet I would often view dates as a waste of time. I let the uncertainty cause me to doubt the dating process.

THE RETURN

Only you can decide if you are ready or if the person is right for you, but there is no guarantee what the return on investment will be. Either it will yield a successful long-term relationship or your return will be life lessons that you can benefit from in the future. However, do not view it as a potential loss, because you won't win with that mindset. Whenever you take a chance, the return may be love or a lesson, but don't view it as a loss.

SELF-REFLECTION

How do you know when a relationship is right? How do you know when you should take a chance? Do a risk vs. reward test. List the characteristics of the person you want in your future along with your other non-negotiables. How can you manage your investment if things are going in the wrong direction? Be honest with yourself and be real.

NOTES

Notes

CONTENTMENT

Will your life end if you never get married? Are you considered a failure if you don't have children? The answers are no, so don't let your current circumstances create chaos for your future.

As alpha females, we put time and effort into our lives, and we enjoy the fruits of our labor. We are also planners. We are taught to put at least five years into our careers before starting a family. However, what happens when five years turn to ten and then twenty? Not only do we have society's pressures but also unmet goals. We then dread going around family for the holidays because we know we will hear, "When will you settle down and get married?" or "When will you have a baby?"

However, neither marriage nor motherhood is in your control, so enjoy life during your journey and wait patiently.

THE JOURNEY

One of life's most challenging aspects is not knowing exactly what God has planned for you. Wondering whether or not He's prepared for you to be married is hard enough, but when you throw the question of children into the mix, it can be easy for anxiety and fear to take over your heart and mind. The best thing to do is not let societal pressures or loneliness cause you to make impulsive decisions. It's not easy to watch your girlfriends get married and start a family, but don't feel less about yourself because you were once on the same path as them. Decide to be happy, because things could be worse.

FOR WORSE

I remember being so upset about gaining weight one time. I lost that weight but, later on, gained it back, plus more. At that point, I wished to be the size I once dreaded because it was better than my current weight. This lesson taught me to be content and grateful that things aren't worse. Comparatively, it would help if you viewed your relationship status the same. Is it better to be single or married and feeling lonelier than you did while single? Do not yearn for what you don't have, but be happy where you are today.

SELF-REFLECTION

Don't resent your current situation; practice gratitude instead. Write down three things you are grateful for each day, and think about those things when anxiety kicks in. No one has the answers or perfect situation; enjoy your life at each phase.

Notes

NOTES

Section III

Attract the Love You Deserve

I am grateful to have been loved and to be loved now and to be able to love, because that liberates. Love liberates. Love says, 'I love you. I'd like to have your arms around me. I'd like to hear your voice in my ear. - **Dr. Maya Angelou**

LOVE & MARRIAGE

Love is patient and kind; love does not envy or boast; it is not arrogant or rude. It does not insist on its own way; it is not irritable or resentful; it does not rejoice at wrongdoing, but rejoices with the truth. **- 1 Corinthians 13:4–8a (ESV)**

Are you ready for love? What kind of love are you looking for? In order to get what we want, we must first understand what it is that we desire.

DATING ON PURPOSE

The purpose of dating is to get married. We don't date to see what happens. Once we decide someone is a potential mate, we must align our expectations with theirs. When a man chooses you, it should be because he sees you as a partner and because he loves you.

Understanding the different types of love can help us to better examine our current love life and see where we may need to make some changes. Let's break down four types of love in the bible to ensure we pursue the right kind of love for the right reasons.

FOUR TYPES OF LOVE

Eros: Erotic love. The way a man and woman passionately love one another. This type of love drives us to seek out a partner.

Philia: Brotherly love. The way we love friends, our peers/equals, or those similar to us.

Storge: Family love. The way we love our parents, siblings, or close family members.

Agape: Unconditional love. Godly love. The way we love humanity. Love that is given, whether deserved or reciprocated. It says, "I love you regardless of how you treat me."

Although agape love should be in the other three types of love, this book is based on eros—relationship love that comes with affection and passionate desires that a man and woman have for one another. Attraction and romantic feelings are essential when considering someone for marriage. Sex is a part of marriage, so sexual chemistry must be there.

What's Your Reason

For some people, marriage is a contract between two individuals to have and raise children. If you desire marriage so that you can become a mom, then the love you are craving is storge, and marriage will not give you that. Your biological clock is not the right reason to get married, and there are no guarantees you will have children.

Others prefer to marry friends because it feels "safe." They won't get their heart broken; however, this can lead them down an unhappy path when pursuing love during the course of their relationship. Although friendship is great for starting off relationships, if both parties don't feel a romantic connection, the original friendship could lead to resentment in the future.

Why Get Married

Love can be a tricky thing to navigate through life. It's important not to get married just for the sake of filling other voids in your heart or because you think it will make up for something that is missing. You can't replace one form of love with another, because they each have their own purpose.

The love from my husband cannot fill the lack of love I received from my dad, because my husband's love was meant to be passionate and different from any other relationship. When you are choosing a partner for marriage, it's important that you love and accept him just as he is (agape). You also have to enjoy spending time with him and doing things you both like (philia). Most importantly, your love must say, "I want to share my life, body, and bed with only him."

SELF-REFLECTION

What kind of love are you looking for? What type of love do you have right now in your life? If the answer is not the love that you want, it's time to make a change. Position yourself to attract and receive the love that will fulfill you in the long run. Remember, it all starts with self-love!

NOTES

Notes

Love Is Blind

Now to Him who is able to do exceedingly abundantly above all that we ask or think, according to the power that works in us. **- Ephesians 3:20 NKJV**

What caused you to give up on finding true love? Was it your mother's second divorce or your grandmother's lifetime of loneliness?

As daughters, we learn a lot from our mothers and mother figures. It's easy to believe in obtaining a master's degree if our mother has one. Comparatively, it is hard to expect a loving relationship if we have never seen one at home.

We cannot allow ourselves to block out love because of the relationship pain experienced by mothers or others. The absence of happy marriages can cause doubt, because it's hard to visualize having something you've never seen. If our mother figure never had it, it's easy to think we won't, but everyone's situation is different. To receive the love you deserve, sometimes you have to go into it with blind faith.

To keep an open mind, you must pay attention to the patterns you may have witnessed subconsciously. Whether you saw your mother crying at night because your father didn't come home or you saw the exhaustion on her face because she raised you without your father, you do not have to experience the same thing. Let your mother bear her burdens, and prepare to do better and receive better. Don't use another person's life as a reason to avoid pursuing what you want. Don't take on their pain and fear the same fate. Although it's difficult when what you've seen with your eyes is the opposite of what's in your heart, keep faith in God.

You deserve love and can have what you desire. In order to attract the love you desire, you need to believe you deserve it. Instead of meditating on those who became depressed following failed relationships, look for the happily ever afters. Give your brain a fresh start. Ask God for help and to place people with healthy relationships in your life who you can learn from. Then visualize your happy ending. This will position your mind and body to have a healthy relationship with a man. Don't bring your mother's or grandmother's baggage into a new relationship. By changing your perspective and taking time to visualize the relationship you want, you can open yourself up to new possibilities for love. God created you, and He knows the desires of your heart. Pursue the love you've always wanted, because it is what you deserve.

SELF-REFLECTION

It's essential that you visualize a long-term love relationship. Seeing is believing and if you can find examples of healthy marriages to observe, it will help change your perspective. How can you go about changing your past view on marriage? Position yourself so that you are the one in control of your thoughts and emotions. Change begins with YOU!

NOTES

Notes

READY TO LOVE

Love is not proven by factual data. No exam can give us a 100% pertaining to love. So, how will we know?

As alpha females, we measure success based on a lavish lifestyle, but love can't be measured that way. Love is not a physical attribute that can be displayed. This can be troublesome for us. To be ready for love, we must be open to accepting and trusting someone else to love us. I know firsthand.

When I was single, I met several nice men, but I would sabotage my relationships out of fear of heartbreak later on. Was I loveable? Could he love me? Why does anyone love me? Those are the questions I had inside, which caused me to doubt that I was worthy of receiving love.

RECEIVING LOVE

Love is first a decision, then a feeling, followed by actions. For me, it was easy to love my husband, because I truly adore him. However, it was a process to trust his love even though his actions showed me that I could. From the outside looking in, anyone could see his adoration for me. Although I could see it, too, I had to accept it and not worry about the future based on my past.

My husband is not my ex-husband, and he is not my father either. No matter what went wrong in the past, it has nothing to do with the future. Focusing on the great things about me created a safe place for my husband to love me, and it helped me to trust that his love wouldn't disappoint. Although it didn't happen overnight, and I'm still working on receiving his love unconditionally even a year after marriage, I committed to perfecting my love for myself, which made me ready for my husband to love me.

SELF-LOVE

Although you should have worked on your self-love and written down the things you love about yourself, sometimes, in the dating pool, the competition is fierce and can cause self-doubt. However, the way we keep our job resume updated is the same way we should keep our personal resume updated.

MY RESUME

I am a great daughter, mother, and friend to others, but I had to intentionally focus on what I loved about myself. I had to love my smile, my physical appearance, my intellect, and who I was as a person.

Instead of doing things out of habit, I learned to thank myself for doing what I would admire if I saw others do it—doing good deeds for my aging mom, supporting my adult brother through his challenges, parenting my adult children, being available any time of the night for my girlfriends, financially helping others in need, and so many other great things. I wrote down all those things to refer back to later so I could remember why I loved me—from smiling at people in the drive-thru to supporting others when they are being recognized and inviting others over for holidays so they won't be alone. Those are all admirable qualities that I learned to love about myself.

Focusing on my positive attributes made me like being with myself. That meant it was okay if I was alone because I was in good company with myself. Spending time with Christal helped me receive love from my husband without so many doubts. Although it was not easy, because I was hurt in the past, reminding myself what I love about myself and what I stand for is what helped me to receive love from my husband.

SELF-REFLECTION

It's important to admire yourself, because you will believe you are worthy of others' love.

What's on your resume list? What are some of the benefits you bring to your family and friends? Why do you love you? Reflect on all the beautiful things you have done for others, write them down, and meditate on them.

NOTES

NOTES

THE MATCHMAKER

Being confident of this, that He who began a good work in you will carry it on to completion until the day of Christ Jesus. **- Philippians 1:6 KJV**

If it's not working, then make it work. If it's still not going well, find something better. An optimistic mindset fuels alpha females for professional success. What about optimism for personal success?

As alpha females, we are determined and confident in our ability to perform at work. We can walk into a room and own it. Why? Because we put the time into our careers, and we know that our more than 10,000 hours and ten years confirm we are experts, influencers, and leaders.

When it comes to our careers, we have it down to the number of hours and years, which gives us confidence and comfort in our endeavors and future endeavors. We know we are worthy of achieving our goals, so we are not afraid to invest in our professional development or network for new opportunities. We are optimistic about our future, whether it's a salary increase, pension, autonomy, or financial freedom with early retirement. Yet, we doubt our ability to meet the right man due to age, status, statistics, or negative baggage from past relationships. What we are questioning is our worthiness to receive love.

Doubt on the inside diminishes your value on the outside. You deserve a great partner because God created you perfectly, and He said goodness and mercies would follow you all the days of your life. If you feel unsure about your worth, then it will show, and you will not be able to own a room full of single men. Strive to have confidence in your ability to be loved as a wife. You are worthy, whole, and complete, and you are not looking for someone to complete you.

Remember all of the things you love about yourself and all of the beautiful things you do when no one else is looking. You love yourself, which makes it easy for others to love you.

God is the master creator and matchmaker. Be confident in His work.

ATTRACT THE LOVE YOU DESERVE

To win at love and attract the right person, seek God always, and have hope in His goodness. Then your inner thoughts will give you the confidence to shine bright on the outside and attract the love you desire. The best version of you is the confident you who knows you deserve love. Walk with confidence, knowing that God is on your side.

SELF-REFLECTION

How would it feel if you were optimistic that your time investments in love would yield a twenty-five-year marriage at age sixty-five? Would you be more willing to network to meet the right man or invest in yourself so that when you met the right person, he would meet the best version of you?

NOTES

Notes

Love at First Sight

"This is the last time! If this does not work, then I'm done!" Are you telling yourself that this is the last time you will try at love? Or are you all in, regardless of not being able to predict the future?

Big Dreams Big Hope

As alpha females, we may leave a job or situation for a better opportunity. We do what's necessary for the big picture and the long run. We don't give up on financial freedom because we change careers or begin new ones; we find ways to improve by surrounding ourselves with other successful women, and we network to meet new people and gain more opportunities for the future. Yet we feel like giving up on love if it's not working after a relationship ends.

We have to keep striving the way we do in our careers, no matter if we have to find a more suitable mate or not. It's possible that you could go from a breakup of a ten-year relationship to love at first sight. Keeping faith until you achieve your goal is essential.

DO NOT SETTLE

Love can be frustrating, because we are not guaranteed a definite outcome from each relationship. However, if we do not control our emotions, then our disappointments can be damaging to our mental state, leading to hopelessness and ultimately settling for what we don't want.

Assigning our potential mate a list of realistic controlled variables is a good thing. It's okay to revisit and revise your list, but don't abandon it. Many women end up unhappy because the men they chose to marry fell extremely short of what they originally wanted.

As alpha females, we do not settle in our careers; therefore, relationships should be no different. We may not be able to predict the number of hours it will take for love to happen or how many tries, so we must control the things that we can manage such as what we desire in a partner. Don't lower your expectations out of fear of being alone. If you have a Ph.D. and desire a college-educated man, reducing your educational requirement for a drug dealer with multiple felonies is not the answer.

I heard someone say she prays every night that God sends her the right man. However, she contradicted herself when she said, "But any man will do at this point." Those statements come from fear of not getting what you desire. It's hard when you feel you've waited so long. The solution is to speak exactly what you want to manifest and meditate on the time or pain it takes to manifest. When negative thoughts come to your mind, use your words to overpower them. Whenever you are thinking something and you speak, then those thoughts go away the same way that darkness goes away when you turn on the light switch. Next time your thoughts are not in line with your heart, take authority over your thoughts with your words. What you say out of your mouth will manifest in your life. God can move suddenly.

SELF-REFLECTION

What are you saying about your love life? How can you turn your negative thoughts and words into positive affirmations?

NOTES

NOTES

REALITY CHECK

A prudent man foresees evil and hides himself, But the simple pass on and are punished. **- Proverbs 22:3 NKJV**

Are you being catfished? Does "plenty of fish" mean you are one of many? What do you use to determine if a man is being genuine or not?

Covid has stopped people from being outside, and it's clear that online dating apps have been on the rise for years. Meeting people online may be a thing right now, but it's important to distinguish reality from falsity.

Men still must do the pursuing online, although women are making themselves available by having profiles. It's natural for men to pick the women they want and then narrow it down. Although men are the ones who ultimately choose women, and women take the men's last names, you still have to protect yourself from being fooled and not let him control everything. It would help if you established an online standardized practice—such as, how long will you wait before seeing him for the first time? How do you know he isn't a serial killer so you're comfortable meeting him in person? How will you verify his identity while remaining safe? Those are the questions you have to ask yourself. The beauty of online dating is that there is so much information for you to cross-reference. Therefore, do your homework and always share your online dating with people you trust to get an unbiased point of view.

PICTURE PERFECT

I know someone who was virtually dating a guy for four months, and she never saw him or even a video of him. When I heard this, I immediately thought this guy was fake. Seeing still pictures and voices on the phone is not enough to verify someone's identity. You have to match the voice with the face in the picture. Nowadays, we all have video apps we can use to speak with someone. Therefore, it is a red flag if you haven't had any face-to-face interactions via video. I recommend seeing someone via video first before going out in person.

PROFESSIONAL PROFILE

As alpha women, our information is easy to find online because we are proud of our accomplishments. You can find us on social business sites where our employment can be verified. You can see us tagged in events and pictures with other people. We even get endorsements that can be cross-referenced. Therefore, his public, professional profile must align with what he says he does for a living. Some men come after alpha women for financial benefits, so do your due diligence to find someone equal to you.

The virtual world has brought together some beautiful relationships. However, it has also exposed lies told by others. If this is a route that you pursue, then have a checklist or standard operating procedures that you will follow. It's always good if you can also find a mutual person that knows both you and the person you met online. Thus, incorporate standards and trustworthy people to help you as you explore the online dating world.

SELF-REFLECTION

Which dating apps are the safest? Who do you know who got married after meeting someone online? What did they do? What lessons can they teach you to avoid a fake person? How will you determine if someone is honest?

NOTES

NOTES

THE ULTIMATUM

Are you his side piece? To be a man's side piece is to settle for second, third, or fourth place.

We discussed that online dating is on the rise, and there are also reality shows with a pool of people to decide on. It is essential to know your position with a man. Being a side piece is not going for what you want but compromising out of desperation.

SIDE PIECE OR MAIN?

It's important to set expectations at the beginning of a relationship. If you meet someone who is already in a relationship, then they are not available to you. It doesn't matter what qualities they have; don't give the relationship a second thought.

I cringed once when I heard another woman say, "He is so cute, but he's married." That statement is an oxymoron, because if he is married, he is off-limits to your eyes. Whether you plan to steal someone's husband or if you fall for a married man unplanned, it is wrong, and you are sowing the bad seeds in your life. Would you want someone checking out your man? Then every married man is off limits to you.

THE LADIES MAN

Set expectations in the beginning so you do not invest too much time in the wrong situation. Sometimes you may meet a man, and he says he's dating just you. However, when he shows you otherwise, move on. You do not want to be someone's side piece or their main piece; you want to be the only one.

When you know there are other women involved and you stay in a relationship, you are diminishing your value and settling for less. There will always be problems if there are more than two people in a romantic relationship. This is the case now, just like it was back in the bible days. You may think you are giving a man what he wants, but there will be a conflict with the other women and pressure on the man—things will not be optimal.

Sarai thinking it was a good thing to make her husband happy by giving him a son with another woman because she didn't have faith she could conceive is just like you agreeing to have threesomes or be the third or fourth leg in a relationship. The outcome will never be good and will cause problems, resulting in hurt people.

Consequently, Haggar, Sarai's maid, became a single mom because she was the third leg in the marriage. Not only did Saria make it difficult for Haggar, but Haggar conceived a child who would be negatively affected as well.

A marriage is between one man and one woman. If a relationship does not begin with you being the only woman or if it develops into you not being the only woman, then exit the relationship and wait on the Lord to bring your person.

SELF-REFLECTION

How can you trust a man but verify you are the only one? What ethical things can you do, such as meeting his family, going to his place of residence to ensure he lives alone, using social media checks, etc.? It is always best to start on the right track and monitor the progress as time goes on.

NOTES

NOTES

WORK CITED

"Clare Boothe Luce Quotes." *BrainyQuote.com*,
BrainyMedia Inc, 2023,
https://www.brainyquote.com/quotes/clare_boothe_luce_1
05139.

"James E. Faust Quotes." *BrainyQuote.com*,
BrainyMedia Inc, 2023,
https://www.brainyquote.com/quotes/james_e_faust_62119
3.

Vanzant, Iyanla. *AZQuotes.com*, Wind and Fly LTD,
https://www.azquotes.com/quote/1209715.

Winter, Catherine. "A Real Alpha Female Will Have These 9

Characteristics." *A Conscious Rethink,* 1 June 2022,
http://www.aconsciousrethink.com/6758/characteristics-
alpha-female/.

ACKNOWLEDGMENTS

I want to thank my amazing tribe that believed in this alpha female movement from the start.

I have to thank my husband, Adrian Jennings, for pushing me to reach higher.

Thank you to my God-appointed sister Rozonda "Chilli" Thomas, for being a part of this project! Your words were a perfect culmination of our friendship over the years.

I am shouting a huge thank you to Ayanna Mills Ambrose, the most fantastic publishing consultant in the world! I'm so thankful to have connected with you for this project. I look forward to us doing the next one together next year!

Thank you to my editor Sarah Leonard for taking a referral from my favorite writer.

Thank you to my girl Mrz. Shyneka for holding me accountable and creating an opportunity for me to grow.

Thank you, Jamal James and Datrick Davis, for holding a sister down during the rough times and having my back.

Thank you to all my YouTube subscribers who tune in each week for relationship conversations for hopeful romantics like myself. I hope you will continue on this journey with me.

ABOUT THE AUTHOR

Christal D. Jordan is an author, journalist, and professional entertainment publicist with twenty years of experience in celebrity marketing and branding. Her first book, *Under the Cherry Moon*, debuted in 2006, and her sophomore book, *How to Win When Shit Happens*, released in May 2020.

Jordan worked in the corporate PR sector before relocating to Atlanta, GA and founding Enchanted Branding and Public Relations in 2008. The company specializes in public relations strategy, media training/consultation, and crisis communication for notable celebrity talent such as TLC's Chilli, Roy Jones Jr., Kenan Thompson, and more. Furthermore, Jordan serves as a journalist and director for *Rolling Out Magazine* where she specializes in stories focusing on empowering women.

Jordan earned her Bachelor of Arts degree in Organizational Communications and her Master of Arts in Mass Communications from the University of Phoenix. Most recently, Jordan started a YouTube channel pulling from her own experiences with celebrity endorsements and strategic relationships. The channel, entitled *From Christal with Love XO*, boasts over 23k subscribers and celebrates love and relationships from a progressive lens. Jordan has contributed to FOX, OWN, Black News Channel, Revolt, Essence, and Black Women's Health Imperative.

www.ingramcontent.com/pod-product-compliance
Lightning Source LLC
Chambersburg PA
CBHW070902160726
48004CB00003B/1215